HEINEMANN MATHEMATICS 1

Name

WORKBOOK 3
Counting to 10

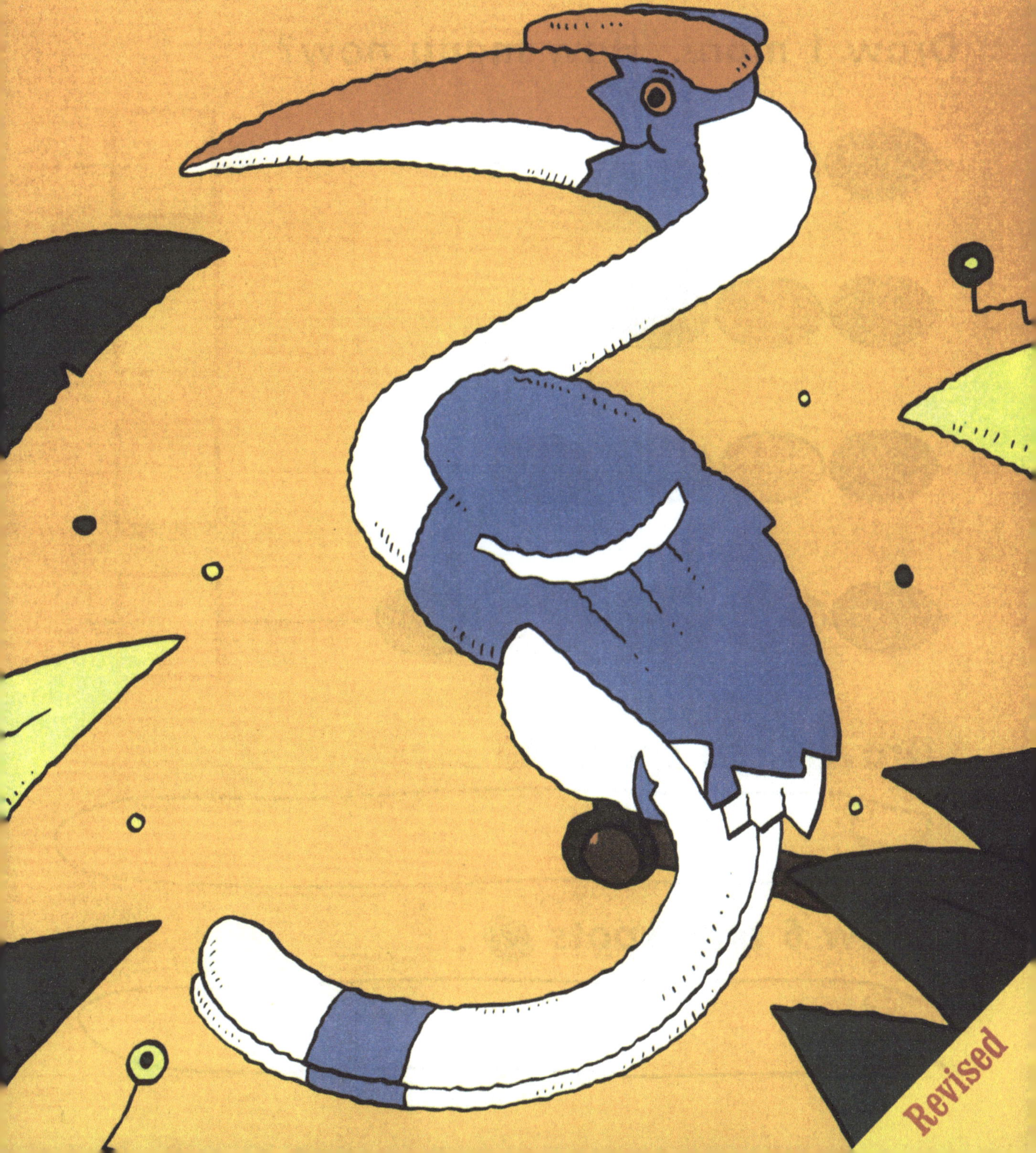

Revised

Counting to 6

Draw 1 more. How many now?

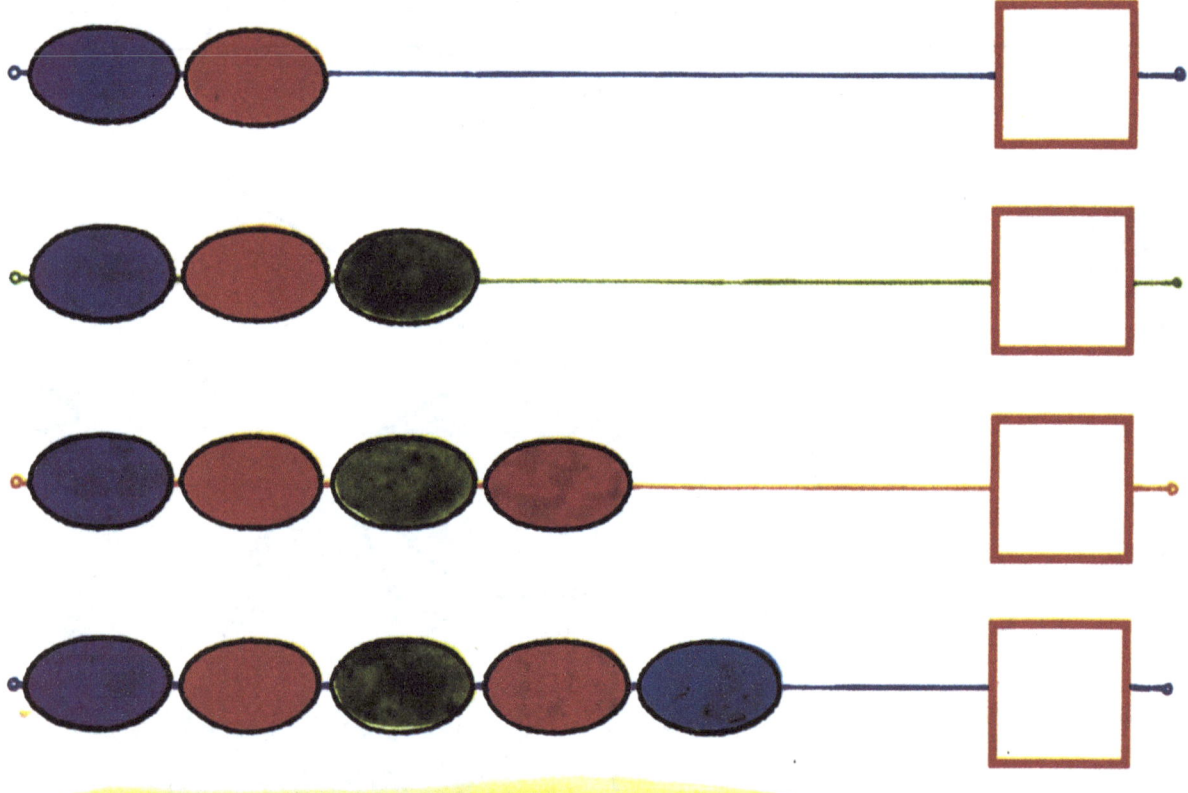

Draw 6 red spots .

Draw 6 blue spots .

How many?

Counting to 7

Draw 1 more. How many now?

How many?

Counting

4

How many?

Tadpoles

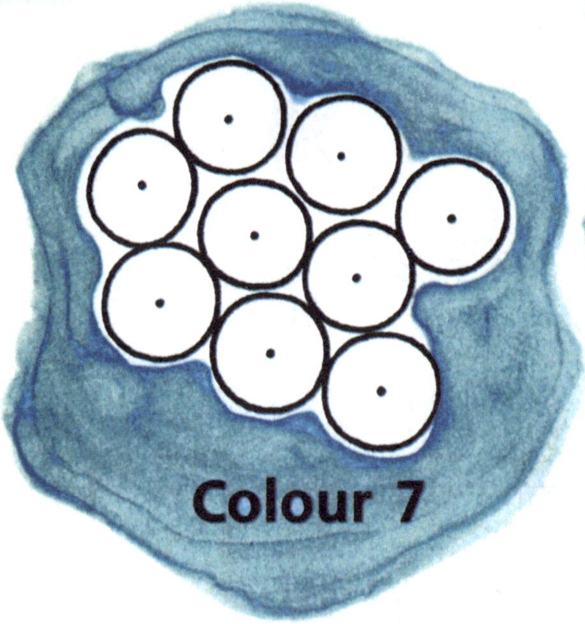

Colour 7

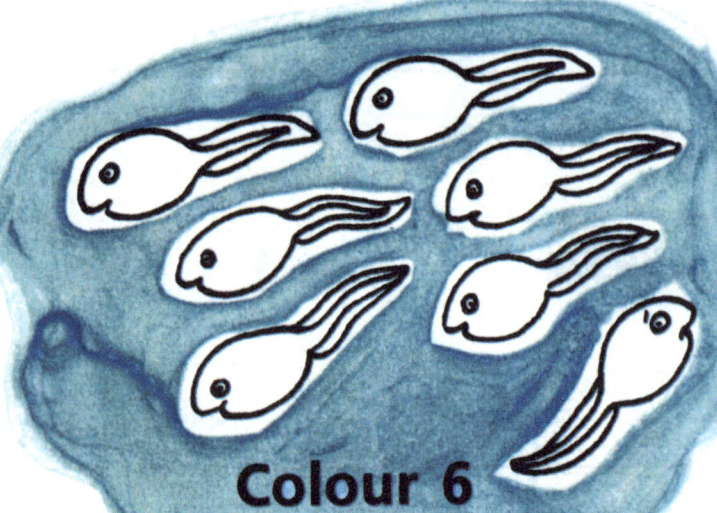
Colour 6

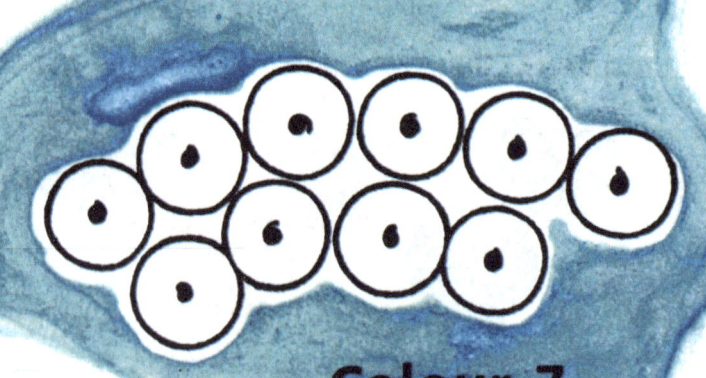
Colour 7

Colour 6

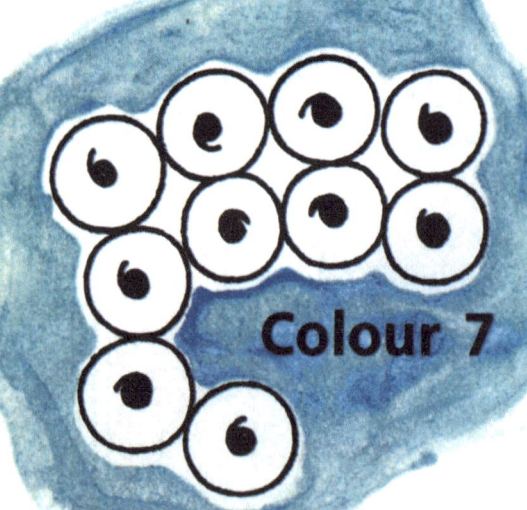
Colour 7

Counting to 8

6

Draw 1 more. How many now?

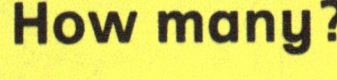

How many?

Counting to 8

How many?

Counting to 9

9

Draw 1 more. How many now?

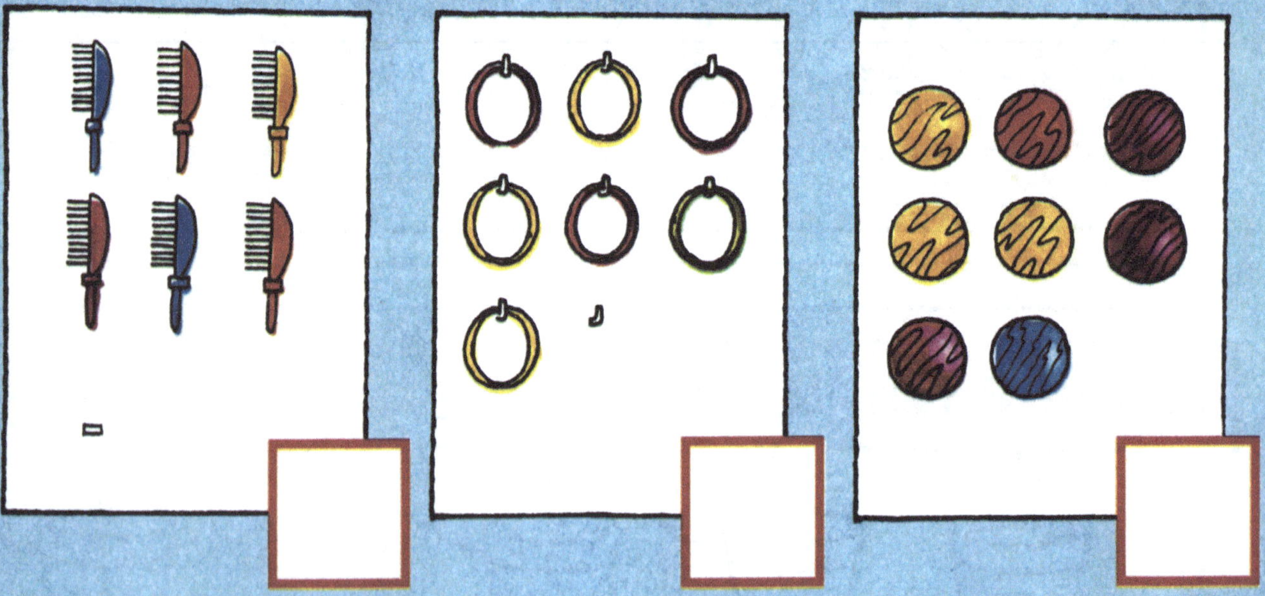

How many?

How many?

Counting to 9

Match

Counting to 10

12

| 10 | 10 | | | | | | |

Draw 1 more window. How many now?

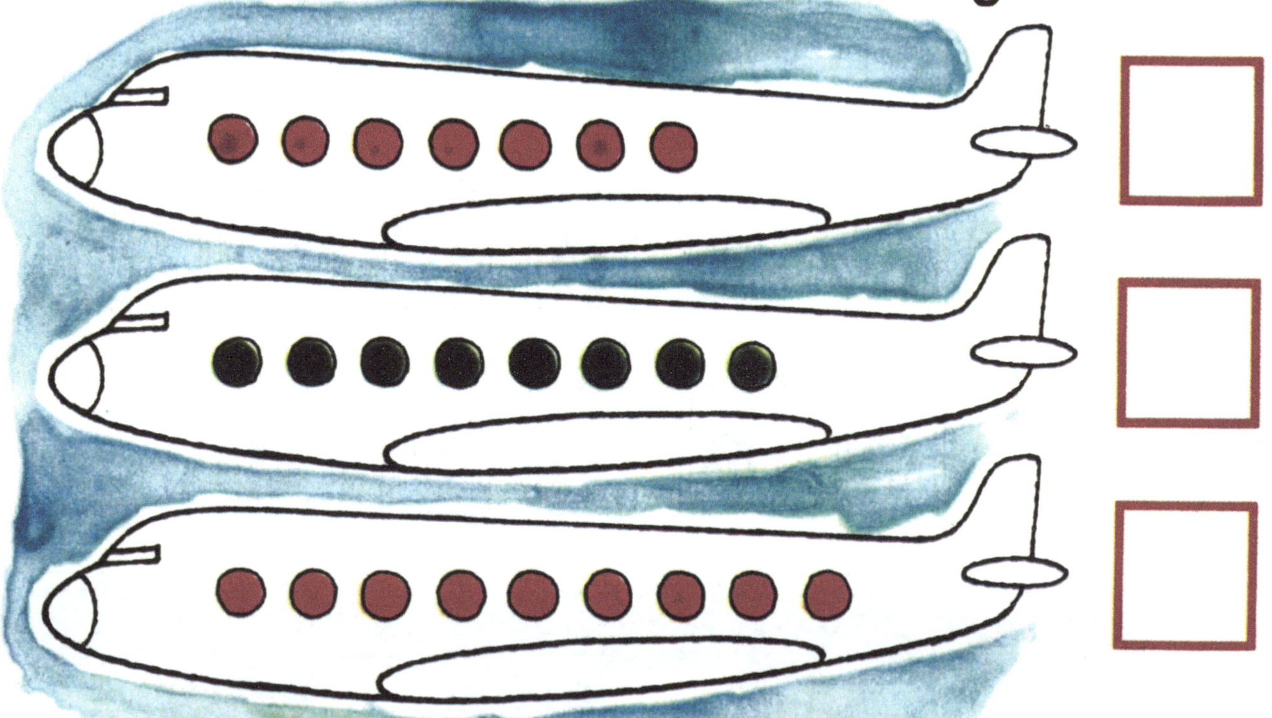

Draw 10 windows.

Counting to 10

Count and colour.

Counting to 10

14

CARDS Counting to 10 Cards 1 to 8

Cubes

Use 9 cubes altogether.
Make this pattern.

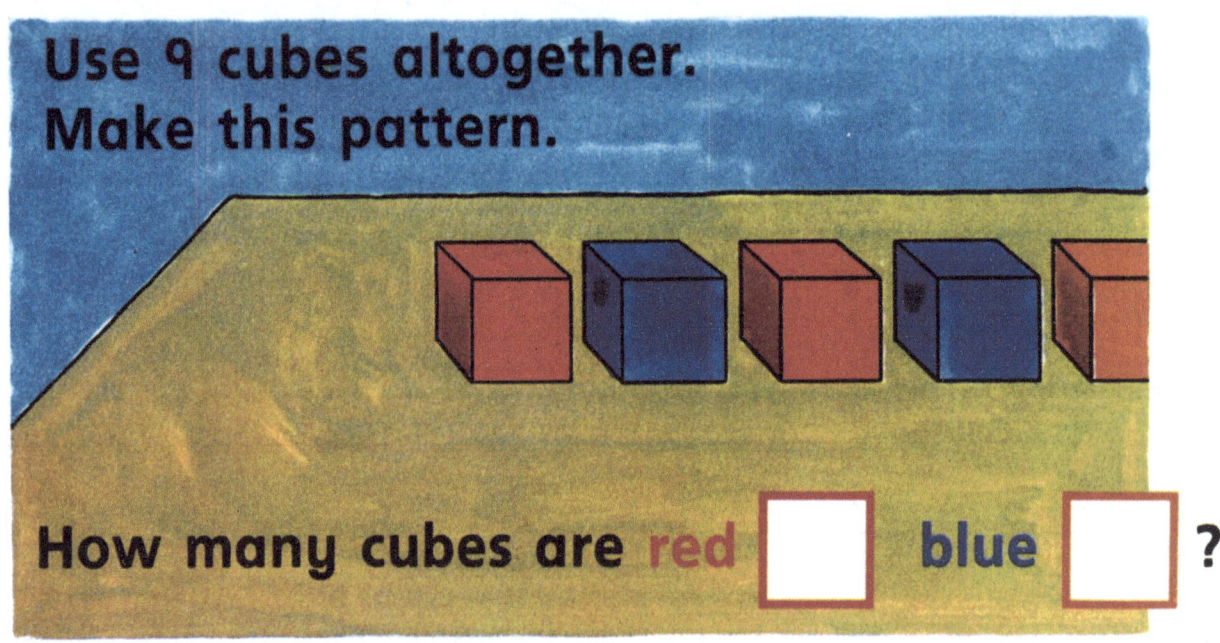

How many cubes are red ☐ blue ☐ ?

Use 9 cubes altogether.
Make this pattern.

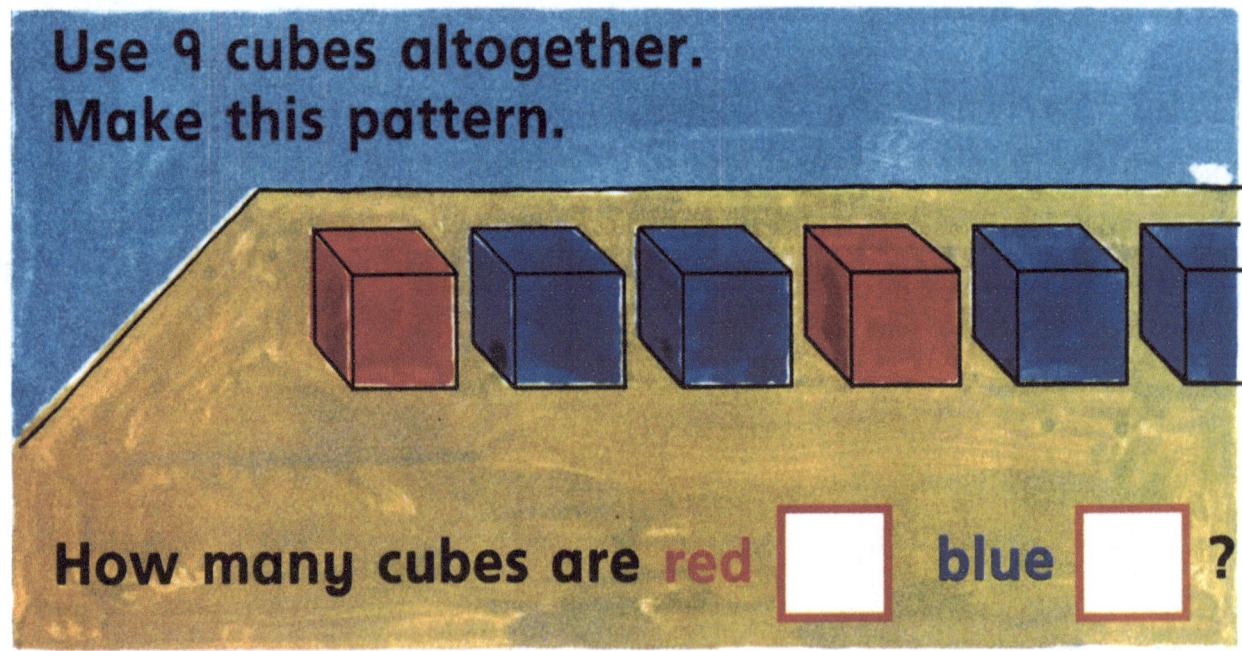

How many cubes are red ☐ blue ☐ ?

Use cubes.
Make your own pattern.